SILT

TRANSMISSION

Transmission denotes the transfer of information, objects or forces from one place to another, from one person to another. Transmission implies urgency, even emergency: a line humming, an alarm sounding, a messenger bearing news. Through Transmission interventions are supported, and opinions overturned. Transmission republishes classic works in philosophy, as it publishes works that re-examine classical philosophical thought. Transmission is the name for what takes place.

SILT

Jon Roffe

re.press

http://www.re-press.org

National Library of Australia Cataloguing-in-Publication Data

Roffe, Jon, author.

Silt / Jon Roffe

978-1-7642346-3-4 (paperback/ebook)

Series: Transmission.

リタへの最後の一冊

My chief concern, in all of this, is to avoid dying in the spotlight of the parental eye.

(Hervé Guibert, To The Friend Who Did Not Save my Life)

Contents

AN ALPHABET IN DISARRAY

Back down the mineshaft again. The darkness is less troubling than during past trips, but there's no quelling the uneasiness at passing the corpses of your previous selves.

§

Beneath your window this past couple of hours—you inside, labouring at the abyssal interregnal task of the translator—two women. Wine, gossip, a sequence about the pronunciation of *arigato*. But then, intermittently, singing, the most astonishing passages from Verdi, Puccini. Suddenly what was above, the second floor, the looming window, becomes the lower ear, the small sub-apartment, the grateful, crouching listener, the *groin*. What else could a body possibly be for than to hear these women? The siren's victims drowned themselves in gratitude.

§

Who *exactly* do we address when we plead 'Please stay'?

§

The mercy of intoxication—being free of the need to remind yourself of your importance. Sadly, it may also amplify the desire to do so. A tricky business.

Further submerge yourself in obscurity.

§

Only a small counter-rotation separates the magnificent nineteenth century hymn 'It is Well with My Soul' from Nietzsche's exclamation in *Ecce Homo*, 'How can I fail to be grateful for my whole life?' That said, you don't need to gaze very far along the extensions of those lines to see that an infinite gap comes to separate them.

§

Scars: closed eyes constantly peering at their origins.

§

Today finds you in the worst of all solitary confinements: the present.

§

The inevitable melancholy terminus of the Anglo-American feast.

§

Beneath the electric hand-drier, the inevitable puddle of water.

§

Energy turns angry when the hands are empty.

Few more concise family histories than the sound of someone's laugh.

§

Life is a disaster. But love ruins life nonetheless.

§

Lesson for writers: habit is a matter of disposition and not momentum, a matter of shape and not motion.

§

Believe in the great Romantic fake-out of spontaneous creativity? Not likely.

§

Tagli. Too afraid to go into a room with them, or any of those *Newmans*, or any of those *Fontanas … what if something gets out?*

Suicide is the abortive attempt to look the accident in the eye—but an attempt nonetheless.

§

Imagine boring your shrink to death ...

Every life is unfinished. Our hope for some kind of resolution, sanctification or stamp of approval comes from our misunderstanding of life. The saying 'life goes on' is correct—at least until it isn't. For each person, to live is to live their ending in its various manifestations.

§

Ah, to be more than a genital wart.

§

The liver, the spirit's lung.

§

Who can arrest the grin sneaking over their chops at the mention of the Platonic slogan 'philosophy begins in wonder'? We continue to grant it a provisional, rearguard status only so long as gives pause anyone tempted to identify philosophy as a hobby ...

Freud and his toys. The mystic writing pad was a mere diversion, an allegory in person rather than the exemplar of the psyche. A manual typewriter hammering new letters into half-dried white-out—this is a truer image of the palimpsest called the unconscious. Another thought derailed by analogy reflux.

Fart jokes, the whole genre of scatological humour leaves you cold. Perhaps your perversion is alliteration instead.

§

The very idea of *belief*: what kind of power do we take this to be exactly? Any completion of the formula 'I believe that …' is redundant. All that was ever at stake was a narcissistic affirmation easily shucked of its alibis. In this, it is the inverse correlate of the formula 'I can imagine …', whose instances are fetishes that obscure the fact that, really, I *cannot.*

§

The sociopath: a pervert looking for an object dressed as a person.

A book of aphorisms is an elaborate optical device, full of adjustable, superimposable lenses, each with its own eccentric loci, focal lengths, thicknesses and strengths.

§

That body listens.

§

The radii of habit's winches are, we must conclude,

often so large to appear to be slight arcs marking out the passage of a life. If we lived longer, their paths would appear true to their circular nature.

§

Today, we are the site of little more than the slack-jawed monetised greebling of organic habits, but for our inability to see this state straïght. To be human is to be a sucker with a lazy eye.

§

Seen from the other end, the smoking of a cigar describes the motion of someone, caught in a moment of ease, slowly plunging face first into hell.

§

Perhaps philosophy is nothing other than an extended effort of making an opportunity out of the crisis of consciousness.

A mixture of necrotic tissue and blood ... the symptom both of anthrax poisoning, and of a body having been alive.

§

The soul is precipitate, black, long-cooked roux.

§

Desire abides in hesitation alone.

Icarus awakens midair, throws up, and begins to fall. He has no recollection of the previous evening, except ... was that his father, upping his bet?

§

The glint in the eye gives it away: there's always some small but significant pleasure to be had displaying your familiarity with the correct pronunciation of proper names. 'sblood. This machine can run on *fumes.*

§

It has proven enough to sustain only the over-distension of the vacant maw of your anxiety.

§

The earth's finite reserves of helium are due to shortly expire. Which element will be next? Perhaps we need a museum of the elements, those defenceless fragments of being.

§

A mediocre poem is a distracted woodcut impression of the poet's character. Hardly a surprise then that such productions are often more enjoyably read backwards.

§

Poetry, like the condom, is an effective prophylactic. Like the condom, its success lies in primarily defending the mediocrity in yourself; like the condom, the poem is only effective in this function some inexact percentage of the time.

§

The Lydian mode. Between the tonic and the sharp fourth yawns desire itself.

§

A short, sharp, dirty thorn, the aphorism.

§

Hell is a noise, not a place: an accident that befalls silence.

§

It's hard to be amused any more with the deathless pleonasm 'see the light'. To not be able to see the light, to strip it from vision in order to confront the darkness in true blindness ... a consummation devoutly to be wished.

§

The baffling, shameless confessions of one Peter Schjeldahl. If your animal spirits incline you towards Koons and away from Bacon, they were surely raised in captivity.

Imagine dying before being able to close a pair of brackets.

§

Poetry … it wakes us up to the fact that we're tied down, makes us struggle at our prisons, even when we can't escape and the struggle only further embeds our restraints.

§

The Voynich manuscript eludes comprehension due to our witless supposition that its mode of functioning is likely benign, at worst mischievous. This is not a coded book of esoteric botany, but an effective instruction manual for the preparation of an ideology.

Alcohol, intimation of indifference.

§

Inarguable, the superiority of the paperback. And yet, it leaves behind a lesson taught by the hard cover, which, from certain angles, clearly appears not as a sheath, protection for the book, but as a holster, that is, a protection *from* the book.

§

True, the apprehension of meaninglessness is most often coupled with despair. But we should not therefore neglect the other things that manifest alongside it: a detached curiosity, a paradoxically conscious blind lust.

§

Amazing, the plasticity of crime. Today a teenage arsonist could genuinely ponder the destruction of an entire nation-state; a regicide could at best aspire to the front cover of the Daily Mail.

§

We must stop distinguishing between critics on the basis of how well they have managed to pre-chew our food.

§

Life, death's wick.

'Midriff' was first the name for what was covered, before it was the name for what was covered.

§

The invention of the earring constituted a transformation in the meaning of jewelry. The necklace, the ring, the anklet all present themselves as suns. But the earring strives to be the immediately obscured eclipse. What we saw but do not see is no longer a thing, but the signature of desire.

There was, of course and by right, not a dry eye in the house. As you left, however, you noticed that your fly was undone.

§

In a conversation, the first impulse of the thinker is to pretend to agree.

§

Mad crowds, rational individuals—snug pair of complementary fantasies.

§

You can't decide whether thinking is the pursuit of life or its infection by death. But its daily experience demonstrates the insignificance of distinguishing the one from the other.

What do our cosmologists, a peculiar contemporary class of heroes of the people, coptering from one TED event to another, actually give to us? Pure genre. Talk of 'the mysteries of the universe', being completely speculative, are as satisfying as digital—calorie free!—ice-cream.

§

Vodka: at once Kevlar and epinephrine.

Bamboo shoots: teenage door meat.

§

In MSG, we find a peculiar mnemic phenomenon, a splitting between the causal function of a salt, and the memorial function of taste. MSG has a double effect, one on each register. This is what explains the particular force of the racist response—*they* are interrupting our way, not just of feeling, but of thinking about what we eat.

§

Salt is the yearning of matter for flavour; MSG is the yearning of food for life.

§

Processed cheese slices approach an asymptote in mechanised production: they are, quite nearly, form without matter. Final triumph of Malévich over Warhol.

The damned drink from whichever barrels are beneath deck.

§

Silt was once the firm ground that supported you, and is now the factor dirtying the waters so you can no longer see anything clearly.

§

The titles of these books of yours get shorter and shorter, while the books themselves grow longer. At the limit, there will just be your name, standing at the front of an unceasing flow of words that try to speak of everything while saying nothing at all.

§

Take someone's photo without consent, you're rightly castigated. But what about these poets with their *pens*?

§

What is called 'night' is just a group of people happening to occupy an especially broad shadow. Standing behind a tree for eight hours would equally do the trick.

Where is the equivalent of music for the skin, the nose, the eyes? If you advert to painting, food and sex in formulating an answer, it's past time you looked for a different book to pretend to read.

§

'The heart wants what the heart wants': a terrifying sentiment. Mute, faceless, it wants in absolute isolation from the world of others ... which of course sounds familiar.

§

The shirt, a curious apparatus, a kind of gamified sack. It continues to surprise you that people keep planting their names on it, like little flags.

§

'I need advice' is a phrase nobody has ever meant ... though it is possible to think of a perversion that involves this drool of the mind, I suppose. For the most part, it is to fear what tears are to grief.

§

You come across a pair of blank spaces in your notebook. With the greatest care, you turn the page. Who can say what combat was waged in order to win that silence?

Why no rainbow of sound? It does exist; we resist formalising it only because it would mean giving the voices of past lovers another listen—their anger, moans, tears.

§

The *dark night of the soul?* Only a marketing firm would have ever called it that.

§

The bottle violates the tenth commandment, according to which the Absolute should never be given material form. Profane proximity of holding and being held.

§

Underwear—what a malapropism. They reflect, more than any other garment, the demands of the outside.

§

'To stamp' and 'to stamp out', a felicitous conjugation.

§

But in the end, names do little more than make an impression and then muddy it—violently.

§

The lamington, Australia in edible form. Bland, sweet, gets stuck in your teeth, it is something that only the tourist should affirm.

§

Fast food, edible advertising, edible static.

§

Quantum physics has taught us that there are no bricks of the world. We must be building our houses with fixations.

§

The idea that writing is transcription—ludicrous. You look away from the world when you write, and draw shapes without referring to anything. Scribe of nothing, apparate!

§

The young man portrays the artist as a young man. The older he gets, the more opaque both art and artist become. Finally, just the river samediffersamediffersamediffers ...

§

Best, all things considered, that Leibniz was wrong. The most significant part of our experience of the world is, horrifyingly, routine trauma. Think about that being in the background all of the time ...

Like every archive, the internet floats atop a sea of dead souls.

§

What a syrup language is. Why not think of grammar as fluid mechanics, of words in terms of relative fluidity, stickiness, viscosity?

§

Need is the hallucination of desire.

§

Ice does not long to be steam. What a workload our metaphors would have if they'd committed to the task. For the most part, they settle for spinning ontological advertising, seemingly motivated by the tropes of the pulp romance novel.

§

Altitude figures disproportionately in our behavioural metaphors. Perhaps the story of the *fall* is worth a second look ...

§

As the Germans have known for hundreds of years, the constitution of a general, abstract category of art unavoidably involves the addition of an 's' to cunt.

Against Aristotle. All is defined by its end, but for the night, which is its own recrudescent beginning.

§

The wearing of furs, the skins of dead animals ... our nostalgia for the sea, once removed, once displaced.

§

In summer, we smoke to invoke the frosts of winter. In winter, we smoke to summon the sun.

§

Nape, cleavage, hip. All these incidental confections drawn from the body mean so much in love. Perhaps the gall bladder once meant something sublime to the broken-hearted.

§

The direct experience of joy is probably unlivable. Not that we would know.

§

A history of pick-up lines would overturn Gibbon.

§

The working DJ is the best reflection of our habitual twilit existence, feeding repeating pre-recorded enthusiasm to a world with its mouth open and its eyes closed, occasionally bathed in light.

§

The end precedes the beginning in everything but the most trivial of senses.

§

Why do we want something else? Because wanting comes before everything else.

§

Nightmare fuel ... is there any other kind?

§

With all of their allegations and ill-fitting quotations, news reports are quickly becoming the worst-written short-form legal documents of all time. Soon enough, the news will just be that grunt that conjoins advertising placements, a cleansing sorbet that tastes like nothing at all. Honestly, it'll be a relief—finally some rest from the smiling, crypto-moralising retro-prognostication we currently have to deal with.

§

Neon lights—the betrayal of illumination by the desire for attention.

Fog—the essential gesture of weather. Obscuration and the refraction of visibility. First fog, and then clarity. The pure visibility of the town planner, architect, modern philosopher and voyeur takes place in an hypothetical world without weather. They would all be troubled by what is diffused by it, with the exception of the voyeur, whose true desire is to not quite to be able to see.

§

Strange to you that nobody seems to wonder why metals are buried underground. All of those subterranean elements that we fashion our world with today do little more than thrust us prematurely into the depths that we will end up joining anyway.

§

Jewellery makes the body: the necklace the neck, the ring the finger, the earring the ear. Adornments? Hardly. They are lamps, microscopes, windows.

§

Those mathematicians who invented zero: did any of them feel an alien chill down the spine, troubled by the thought of what other abysses they may yet open thought onto?

§

A list is a riptide.

The category of sobriety remains a gesture of longing, an attempt to summon a longed-for orthogonal world. If the devil did exist, it might have absented itself from human affairs, with all due haste, out of shame for the paltry sins ascribed to its name. But it would have nevertheless hung around—out of jealousy, for the hoard of evil human beings keep to themselves.

§

Wittgenstein asks how we know which end of the arrow directs us to the target. A foolish hypothetical question. It is the end stained with viscera. No signifier is arbitrary—they are all bound to their referents by blood. There is one god, and its name is violence.

§

In the mirror, there is no mediation. There is only the silent world of perfect contiguity, Leibniz's world but also the world of the serial philanderer, for whom attachment is merely an optical effect and category error.

§

In the sea of books, trust no tide.

§

There has only ever been drinking. Eating is the fantasy of the tyrant.

LACRIMOSITY

Learn to resist the impulse to try explaining who you are—you're bad at it.

§

Imagine thinking that an aphorism was a polite scion of language! It is a betrayal of the communicative function of language so profound that it appears trivial. Then again, this function does not belong to language itself, but to the Church of Personhood.

§

The phantasmatic invocation of 'the light of history' is direct proof that history itself does not exist.

§

'There is enough light.' No. We think sometimes that everything that can be said has been said. But what the word *language* means is that there is always something else that can be said.

§

History is only the syndicated repetition of the crimes of habit and time.

§

The habits of a great many people, these are the reason you keep so many things strictly to yourself. They cannot be trusted with what neither they nor you understand.

§

The meaning of the word 'violence' is always at stake.

§

The genre of advice rests on an attempt to surreptitiously exchange the relative for the absolute while at the same time passing off the absolute for the relative.

§

A book is never the final word, but the attempt to wrench from the body a metastasis.

§

When the assertion of a truth strikes with the force of an unrecognised fact …

§

You finally notice, much too late, your intoxicated sequestration in the narrative form.

§

Daily it all floats off like scum from a diving mammal, the models, the analyses, everything. Never fear: it is this that coats your mouth and tongue, makes it hard

Caveat lector. By the time you'll be able to understand this warning, it is absolutely too late to be careful about anything, let alone reading.

§

'Logistical nightmare'—sublime, unsublimated, oxymoron.

§

If every act of speech implies a response, the demands of the dead become absolute and permanent.

§

The doors to philosophy are closed from the outside—easily. Those attempting to barricade them from inside, facing away from the doors in their effort to enjoy the shadow play that their construction has produced, second-hand, show both their assholes and their unavoidably failed intent. We arrive, after the fact, and catch glimpses of what must have been an astonishing scene—a scene of ... a casino? An orgy? A mass murder?

§

There are no more parasites of decadence. Their contemporary avatars are brittle and unconvincing. Our alternative is the simple gasping, as fiercely as we can, for air. What appears as great is, as a result, only a matter of good publicity.

There are no more monsters. Straight line, triangle, convergent parallels, asymptote, all expressing the plagal cadences of the idiocy of everyday life. The lesson is that there is no geometrical figure for existence. Now, whether you judge this as melancholy news, or on the other hand …

§

A bronchitis that runs down deep into the body, into each part, so that each breath and each word is marked by its presence. If you follow those pipes down far enough, behold the soul—just another redounding pipe, with its concomitant and equally suspect bronchial flatulence.

§

Almost every punctuation mark can be translated into the language of percussion—the flan, the fermata, the ghost note—with the exception of the semi-colon, which is lost in the tidal grip of quality, the equivocity characteristic to melodic unison.

§

Along the tangled paths of thinking, subtraction and rarefaction are easily confused; the coldness of abstraction must be earnt; its facsimiles are easily confected.

§

The bourgeoisie is no longer (how long has it been?)

characterised by the discreet charm of its social graces. Bourgeois being is no longer located in the world but in the body, not in the object, but in the subject, in the posture of the hand that holds the card, in the embouchure. It desires reflection, but of no kind in particular.

§

When everything you say reduces down to the posing of questions, look to who you ask them of, what you already know they will say in response, and the modality of the surprise you express if they say something else.

§

Everything that dies on the west coast is reborn in the 'work' of rock guitarists. At its franchised heart, rock is the elegy of the twelve-year-old boy. This is what explains the universal becoming-sentimental of successful rock bands.

§

Taxonomy is a late-bearing fruit on the tree of fascination—late-bearing due to the paralysing grip of the flower of opinion from which it flourishes, and which delineates the purposes to which it might be put.

§

Disproof of the efficient market hypothesis: Many crave to be hangmen; many crave to be hung.

Rage is the only necessary and sufficient response to so-called euphemisms.

§

To paraphrase the famous, ill-attributed remark about the working mathematician: the liberal is someone who is a nominalist during the week, but who is a nominalist on the weekends.

§

Academia is neurosis written backwards. The anxiety of its constant misspelling only binds its curates to their condition more tightly.

§

There have only ever been parasocial relationships.

§

The signature of many philosophers: the inevitable failure of the occultation of their tastes. To repeat: if a philosopher procludes the question of taste, their shadows are its avatars.

§

Rewrite the history of philosophy in terms of what should be understood by 'out of the corner of one's eye'.

From the point of view of the angel, Jacob was the unforeseen catastrophe—the first real evidence of hope, the first exposure to the possibility of love, to the other absolute of death. Imagine it! To discover the triviality of God while carrying a message in his name.

§

Amusing, this notion of 'taking turns'—or rather its easy ubiquity. Even setting aside the blinding reality of plurality, we talk as if such a thing was possible, the discrete division of time, of decision, of agency, of outcome.

§

So long as the word 'culture' only refers to the high from eating the placenta of the latency period, human existence can remain little more than a faintly epiphenomenal thrush.

§

To speak is to weep; to write is to mark the writing surface ... Whatever speech is, writing is syneresis.

§

Wittgenstein's medicine is effective, despite being a placebo. This is fortunate, for it happens that the illness that afflicts those that attend him is non-existent, and their wet, ill-directed 'activism' further softens on the vine, troubling nobody but those immediately in their presence.

The greater the artist, the more absolute the demand for another art becomes.

§

The cigar is a lizard that has forgotten itself, especially its tongue. Now nothing but skin all the way through, it is content to be placed back into others' mouths, on the proviso that they do not speak while it is there.

§

Bar the insects, the animals of the old poems are all extinct.

§

The new parasites: meta-acronyms. Like all parasites, they only flourish within the bodies of their hosts.

HORIZONS

The air is thin on the terraces of malice, but the occasional visit proves useful for correcting your perspective on pedestrian existence. The same is not true, obviously, of the runnels of envy.

§

The multiply redundant character of existential dread. The experience is doubled by conscious reflection, which it refracts through a thousand other lenses—therapeutic, poetic, forensic. It is tempting, in fact, to consider this dread an alibi for something more profound, more singular, more dreadful.

§

The mirror is the first technology, the technology coeval with human existence itself. Writing is, before anything else, a kind of mirror.

§

As effective as trying to direct a cough to the part of the throat where the itch is.

§

At the wake: all of us dancing drunk with our backs to the quicksand.

The American 'you' accuses; the Australian 'you' obfuscates.

§

We approach one of the heretofore hidden horizons: the copywriting of speech itself.

§

The colossal error of confusing philosophical significance with academic recognition—less than a flick of the wrist is required to unhorse Habermas, starting at this point—a confusion that the modern academy has done all in its power to bring about, an obvious instance of its labour as a capitalist institution, and not—as it may appear—an insignificant one. But the real suckers are the philosophy academics, whose resistance to this identification wanes within months of beginning to receive the lotus-scented wads of cash.

§

A perfectly ordinary death—fucked liver, rent in arrears on a mid-grade city apartment. Colour grading slightly off. The door locked from the inside.

§

With such a lack of ductility and plasticity, survival is the worst habit to form. Blocking the arteries of the self with minimal algorithms of gesture and digestion, it blocks the formation of other, unexpected habitual fulgurations. We can get no stranger now because our selves live in the umbra of the next meal.

The imagination is the bridle and reins of affect.

§

Lest we forget, these particular tools of mastery are mass-produced.

§

Given the impossibility of dislodging the imbecilic belief that images concord with our mode of existence, the least we could strive towards is an equanimity—if not the curiosity and affirmation that would grow us strange and wild!—towards the uncomfortable shunting they evince.

§

Opting for any one of the panoply means of slow suicide is at root an attempt to abdicate agency for the act. It is, consequently, the most faithful means—the half-hearted disbelief in life.

§

Beware! Your world is closer than it seems. The fundamental disingenuity of libertarianism is unconscious, and thereby lacking ingenuity of any kind. This, setting aside their regrettable squawking, accounts for their naive, animal charm—the charm of confusing quality and value, while refusing any and all analogical implication.The liberal's ingenuity, on the other hand, turns around a trick—an effort—to keep both the confected world and the dumb ego in focus at the same time. It would be a novel achievement, were it at all possible.

§

Life is a universal, an absolute moebius strip; death is the ineluctability of its twisting.

§

Ah, our 'reactors', who work to be the subjects of other subjects. Given how wretched we are for the most part, they have earnt the wage for their mediocre sin, for their gentle work codifying through enthusiasm the order of our affects—the charnel is deep and diverse.

§

Halfway between desire and confession, your family of practical nihilists remain, like you, trembling—or is it oscillating? The truth lies in the marriage of the two: the trembling expresses the desire to merely oscillate. Alas. Is there anything more pitiable to discover a romantic when looking for a fuck?

§

What is to be done? Nothing. And yet, consider that full stop, which follows what should be an absolute conclusion.

§

Burn your bridges, by all means—but since you're

worrying about what other people think, take care that you do not, in doing so, burn someone else's.

§

The ease of masturbation perhaps deceives us about the broader difficulty of living.

§

Existence is treacherous.

§

Ah ... the lamentable fixation on the visible, sight, the whole metonymic circus. We might as well be embedded in the hide of a creature whose horrors and existence are beyond diagonal to our own. Tics riding on Being. Except that there is no Being. Only Beings.

§

The obsession with scale—the giants!—is infantile, neurotic. Ah the mathematical, the dynamical!

§

Hard to think the bourgeois polaroids of the world system can get any more disgusting than this, compliance retreaded with an annual asymptotic glow-up, worst kind of stitch up, where you trade in any kind of freedom for a bleached arse, a half-full glass, a January turkey. The sound of a ball on a bat, close to a cultural symbol; glottalisation cues take the place of a sincere gesture. No worries mate. Just sit still at the barbeque, listen to the laptop tell you the fucking fantastic hundred tracks; swallow those untranslatable sighs. Inside someone's letting blood from their thighs, while you sit here and fantasise about burning down suburbs all the way to the horizon, your sunburn little more than a logo. But you can't avoid being tagged as a sponsor, a martyrcide, a joke told just to your liver on the inside. You just spilled your drink. That'll give your family material (for longer than you think. Nice.) Ice you brought's melting on the patio. Sun's setting way too slow. Better this all died two and a half centuries ago. Spit on the bitumen out the front, waiting for the car. It evaporates within a minute, unlike the sun and the laughter.

§

Nationalism is the caul of capitalism, the only ideological context less general than the completely abstract evanescence of money, and the nutritional grist for early education.

§

Writing is disgusting, a low activity, dirtying the writer, whether they know it or not. Why is this? At a first level, this is due to the sincerity of writing implied in the effort to explain yourself. It is disgusting to subordinate yourself to this sincerity, especially when you know that almost nobody ever reads anything, and, when they do, there's a general air of willful misinterpretation. In striving to communicate, you bend the knee to imbeciles; a little Habermas drools inside our minds.

§

The counterpart of this experience of shame is the proud, amused rejection of any demand for explanation. You can't understand me? Fuck you.

§

An affect never hardens into a conviction, but rather crystallises like molten sugar into toffee, easily binding the teeth.

§

The self fantastises, in the first person, about the third person 'one', who undergoes the fantasies on our behalf. The 'one', subject to fantasy, never has a headache; no bandaid is affixed to their spiritual body, a body shaped like an arrow that would become the point of its own target but for the fact that it never arrives at its destination.

§

What is said is not what is meant. At best, the keen listener will observe something based on the degree to which what is said does not coincide with what everyone else says.

§

An 'I suffer' can always be extracted, from the very

margins of every thought, that persistence, that haggard consciousness unable to rise to the level of knowledge or being, but only to register this misery. This registration is a reliable source of a trickle of enjoyment.

LA SERINISSIMA

Could I behold that endlesse height which is
Zenith to us, and our Antipodes
(John Donne, 'Good Friday 1613. Riding Westward')

Midsummer at the world's chapped lip.
From horizon's crack time bleeds into space
Listless afternoons, shirt stuck to my back
Pen stilled, glass aloft mid-sip.
Everything here
Is just what it is. Crisp edges.
No red shift, no woozy palustre.
Hyena, the dry heat,
And those terrible presences
around and above me. No parasol.
I spend myself watching them meet up
Floor and ceiling, sky and sea.
After a year of desultory attempts
to obtain refunds, to think, to write
Of trying to run my needle across
the signal of the world
Another year of embarrassed
naked craving, and its shadow,
the ache to understand,
to drink the world dry of chance.

But here, there is only the sky's
Firm pressure. To become
tactile but empty, here
I breathe an air without promise.

I wake up each morning small,
spend the day not thinking,
a dead coin running crooked around
the blasted crater of the horizon
Send the old words off
to the knackery. Sit still enough
to lure the silence back, to train
the eye to train the mind black.

§

The daily pagan lie of sunrise
still rouses the pangs of belief
But soon the sky starts falling in
And the stars' shocked shouts sound,

Nationless flags falling backwards into eternity
While my flesh clock winds down
And my mind unspools
Into the merciless, parched night.

§

This black ovid sea moan
Is more in me than my so-called family,
my nation-home. My patrons,
not the philosophers of this new cut-rate Rome
But dispossessed pornographers chained
To rocks far off the coast, livers too fucked
To sustain the animals that flock this
Uncrowded manger full of absent saviours.

The horizon's the marriage of a repeated truism
And a hole, a chain with a single link
Monomaniac, the best the little machine
Can do is bleat the cipher 'yes'

Our marriage to the world is only sustained
If we make peace with the lie of its permanence,
And so long as it maintains its indifference
To our existence, keeps its gaze unfocussed

§

Two weeks in. The days have
come unstuck from their names.
The sea, agar growing the orphan things
catenaried together by unseen tidal threads.
Off the coast of Lampedusa
the Madonna di Porto Salvo drowns forever.
She lies with her name, with her gesture
She is everything profane. She mimics
Or mocks our posture of hope.
Suspended, floating in judgment,
purgatory full of wrecks, the past
Poisoning the water.

§

Finally, one afternoon during week three
I am summoned by the hammering of gulls
perforating the bloodshot eye of sunset,
fall windoward, see the world rearing up:
Nothing underway, nascent absence.
A hole in the world in the place
where the world had been.

I slit my mind at the wrist and slip in.

§

To come here each time is to wait
Without hope for the new
Day's year, to be remade
In the image of the world
The world's name is *nothing*
And that name means *begin.*

THE RELAPSARIAN

First tragedy, and then farce, yes ... but *then* what?

§

Slander of Jormundgandr. Since being swallowed whole by the lossless ouroboros, we have forgotten that his tale concluded not once more at the beginning, but at the definitive, frayed, irrecuperable end of time.

§

The rhythm of capitalism is the relapse.

§

Recognition of a lapse directs one's attention to what has fallen back and away. Even the origin of the word itself has fallen back into oblivion.

§

Benjamin mistook the nature of the so-called angel of history. The 'angel' in question, the inverse counterpart of the gargoyle in every respect, only moves when we look back at it. Its true name is Eurydice, the one who, rolling back on her tracks, returns to hell at the slightest glance. History is not a nightmare from which we might awake, but the pastiched imaginary figure we cannot help but try to capture in a glance. History as declined mirror.

Copernicus' house arrest bloomed from a colossal laziness. At least somebody ought to have paid attention to the ubiquity of the straight line. Hence the double sin of the 'common sense' rejections of heliocentrism—to confuse the evidence of perception for the truth of celestial reality is to make a confused heaven of a blighted earth.

§

Poetry flourishes under the sign of eternity, but the horizon of philosophy is time.

§

The true everyman is not doublebound Hamlet but witless Horatio—best prepared to mourn disaster retrospectively, drunk on the near-fermented tragedy sipped from the fertile depths of others' bodies.

§

To starve oneself—why not? It appears like the antithesis of the ubiquitous, empty imperative: consume. Except that it too is—in this relapsing mode of sociality—a form of consumption, and thus a form of obedience.

§

Kierkegaard opines that faith sees best in the dark. But like the ring returned to him from that fateful broken engagement, his darkness only ever belonged to him. He only erroneously infers its general existence to lie beneath the unremitting light of being.

§

Because of the subtle and various ways in which it affects every dimension of being and existence, modernity threatens the thinker with its apotheosis. For thought in its unreflective spontaneity, it can appear natural; but thought in its critical reflexivity, it can appear necessary. Until it is grasped, for all of its vast and plastic powers, as contingent, it is not grasped from the modern point of view. It is the category of history itself that is at issue—does it name the texture of time, or is it an alibi for its permanent counterpart?

§

Neither prospect nor retrospect grasp the character of a revolution.

§

History, the mirkin we paste onto the past.

§

Because each instant is a larval disaster, the whole of one's life is at stake in every moment. Beneath the mediatic roar, we save and damn each other over and over again in the silence of our gestures and in the spaces between our words.

Swollen shut like a window; swollen shut like an analogy.

§

Adolescence gives the lie to the idea that empiricism arises from the contradictions of rationalism. An eccentric narcissism (is there any other kind?) is the least of our problems. Perpetually re-resurrected, our belief in intellectual intuition—the unkillable kernel of rationalism, narcissism and spontaneous empiricism alike.

§

The latency period certainly explains the plastic structure of consciousness; it also provides the structure—endemically paternalist—to morality.

§

Hope is an horizon internal to consciousness. Like every horizon, it is relative to its context. But—what if there is more than *one* horizon?

§

Note the similarity between the posture and glazed eyes of the daydreamer and those of the dead. Death—permanent distraction.

Hope is the congenital overbite of the human spirit, preventing all of our teeth from ever coming to bear on the present at the same time.

§

'Avoid any philosophy that pulverises the given'—but why? It pulverises us.

§

A good lover is always on the side of the future; so too, unfortunately, is a cruel one.

§

The awful yawning of time that puts the lie to every uttering of the present.

§

The form of the story is soporific—or at the least, anaesthetic. This is the kernel of Marx's diagnostic of religion, but it remains, at a deeper level, the kernel of certain Marxist tales about the nature of history.

§

It is not your tinnitus, but the tinnitus of being. At once a lure—are you hearing something, or just your own broken stereoscope?—a meaningless hum, oscillating according to principles you are unable to discern, and the mark of a trauma unregistered at the time of its occurrence, which is to say a trauma as such.

The tonic may long to return to the tonic. It is because it must do so by way of we who hear it—the faithless ones, foreign and lost to ourselves—that it necessarily loses itself in turn, sounding a fraction off, unable, in its groping to clasp together its now chiral hands.

§

Evidence for the non-isomorphism of time and space: there is no temporal equivalent of vertigo, but for time itself.

§

To be melancholy is to have fallen only halfway to joy. The relevant advice—untangle your little finger from the tapestry of 'fate', fool!—goes unheeded, for the precise reason that the melancholics take themselves to be stroking the velveteen undergarments of the heavens, having mistaken the fall for an asymptotic ascent.

§

God, but that you had been granted the capacity to distinguish rhythms from those fatal recursions that do not rhyme.

DDoS

Ah, falling stars. They provide us with a clear measure of our hubris, given our constant allegation that they 'fall to earth', a phrase we ludicrously use even while we're watching them stream past us. Stars move at their terminal velocity; they fall to earth only if terminally ensnared in the Earth's well of gravity. Their destiny derailed, they will become cellphone components.

§

The liver is the real sin against the spirit.

§

Everything we get, we deserve—except for the times we get. Life is the blind victim of rhythm, at the very moment that rhythm blinds life to this temporal subordination. We misconstrue our habits as our possessions, when they are our shackles.

§

The beautiful fiction of explanatory parsimony. Ockham—if that really was his name—forgot that an effective razor has blades on both sides. I leave aside the question: minima of *what*?

§

1. Distinguish between desire and its fervid atmosphere to discover the coldness of desire, its structural character. 2. New question: is the coldness of desire

itself an atmosphere? Can a structure be composed of pure affect? Surely, yes. 3. During the pursuit this question, the fervidity of desire passes over into the activity of questioning. Is questioning just a case of desiring? So long as we don't make the mistake of identifying desiring-questioning with the desire for an answer—yes. 4. The issue is not so simple as that. What explains the emergence of an object of questioning? This object is the *sine qua non* of questioning, even though it seems to be strictly and in principle unobtainable on its own terms. 4a. First hypothesis. The object cannot itself be desire, at least if questioning can be equal to it. This would dissolve the object back within the general movement of desire and mean that either questioning has no terminus (no need to declare *hypothesis non fingo!*). 4b. second hypothesis, hypothesis *a tergo*. 5. Notice that the earlier question concerning the origin of the object of questioning was skipped over. This whole investigation has begun to spiral out of control, as it so often does. 6. Does it *always* spiral out of control? Identify the structural character of desiring-questioning with the spiral, rather than the *circulus vitiosus* qua qua qua qua qua …

§

Ideology presupposes the dissimulation of necessity.

§

Homonymy is possible thanks to the dust of language, the thousand clumsy missteps. But this dust, uniquely, possesses its own power to reassert itself within language use, deranging the sense of words.

At the door to death, and at all of the intermediary doors before and thereafter, small communities, whose kernel was fear, grew. Newcomers encountered, not choices, but habits, easily adopted, adding, one at a time, another suburb to the threshold. Now, there is only talk of doors and thresholds, of change, while the real estate agents of these accretions grow fat on the rent.

§

The body is a candle. Ethics is the practice of managed burning. But do not let its practice lead you to forget—there is only burning.

§

Advertising has always been there, always mounting the curb of the soul and its unsuspecting leg at the same time.

§

Can blind affect combat blind affect? The qualification is obviously unnecessary, but remember how we burnish our scars to look like medals.

§

The imagination, bounded by the semi-permeable membrane of the senses, is first of all an invasive site for advertising.

There is no door with only one side. Foucault imagines a beautiful scene - when the time comes to die, you hire out a suite in a suicide hotel. All of your friends come, an amazing time is had. And then, when nobody is looking, you slip away behind a slender, otherwise unnoticed door. But—if you wander, months and years of your life, alone, down dim alleys, silently, or while scraping an idiolect from the pavement, looking for a truly blank piece of paper or a homophony of souls, you'll arrive at the same place, the same near side of that anonymous door, itself on the near side of the absolute end.

§

We know by now that most states of sleeping include some minimal perceptual awareness of one's environment. And yet we continue to put mirrors in our bedrooms. Do I need to make it any clearer? There are absolutely times during which you are *watching yourself sleep.*

§

In your teens, you offered to teach a friend chess, and lost to them in their inaugural game. A bad precedent.

§

What we require is not a characterology, a typology of representations, in the cinema. It presents us with new forms that require their own ethology, the study of the behaviour of the condensed images we call characters.

Jump cuts: the minor, high fructose corn syrup-induced strokes of the cinema.

§

Sobriety is not a state but a scene.

§

The secretary of the regiment. Establishing a definitive list of what you hate is impossible; the making of a list itself quickly becomes questionable. But does this also hold for a list of lists?

§

Caveat aspirans. Constructed beings are mostly fair-weather golems, liable to fall to earth, along with their 'righteous' fury, in the face of a light breeze. The animation of the inanimate is not so easily maintained.

§

The menace once possessed by Kafka's 'Before the Law' has all but evaporated. It can now almost be read as an example of the pinnacle of personalised custom service. As for the formerly sinister Odradek, you heard the other day he was employed as a butler at a country club.

§

A good translation is a modulation of the translator's terror, a terror that is not the fear of inaccuracy but the ongoing threat of an absolute failure. A bad translation follows from the decision to dissolve this terror in the base of narcissism.

LONG DIVISION

I asked for nothing; you tried your best.

§

Years ago, a friend went through a difficult break-up with an aspiring actor. Just as they passed the point of no return, she got work modelling lingerie, and each day he took the train into the city for work, he saw her, immense, staring off into the middle distance, the looming shadow of their past cast over his solitary present. I realise now that every break-up has this form, but for the fact that the surface on which your indifferent glamour is projected is the pernicious surface of the mind.

§

I always wondered what you were staring at instead of looking at me. I have come to understand that you were fixated, not on your phone, but on a future from which I has been erased.

§

Your memory frails my one thin string and makes a drone of everything.

§

Your cold indifference approached that of language itself. This is a truism I tell myself whenever I think of you, in an attempt to make the best of it all, in order to burnish my pride as a writer, with my bile and the cloth of your memory.

§

I felt her silence like the pure presence of time—by which I mean that being in her company felt like being dead.

§

Worst of all, the feeling of *false flight,* of lurching awake, whenever she disappoints me. These were flights to nowhere, since these disappointments followed from her absolute indifference.

§

Hers was a cut so clean I had trouble finding any memory of it afterwards.

§

The signature of our sheets told a compound truth that my simple lies ruined, ruin.

§

Make no mistake: those last months were not the result of cowardice or fear. A week to forget you as a lover, a week to conceive of you as my whetstone, and then a handful more weeks to sharpen my desires for my next victim.

The lure and its reflection—She had polished herself up to such a sheen, habituated a posture such that, given the condition of the light, she could render herself completely reflective, a mirror. To look at her was only ever to look at yourself.

§

Everything I wrote about her immediately took on the character of having been written years afterwards. Fearfully, I went to lock the door—but I paused too long. I stand there still.

§

S would rather starve to death than have P ever recognise them when they see them ever again. Futility—I should have learnt by now that there is no fleeing my predicates, nor any attracting any others.

§

This relationship's combustion would free this song ... I engaged in a constant calculation. If there is only music, and no God, then how much is permitted? What music must I fear might catch fire?

§

A fine pair, you having always already given up on sex, while I, like an inept lawyer on their first case, strive to defend it from the very lip of hope.

Lovers on the ninth ring of hell, we began blind, each of us gradually convinced that we were becoming able to see—license enough for both of us to accuse each other of the worst sins we could think of. Betrayer. Murderer. Beloved.

§

It is beautiful, the first complicity between skin.

§

Lovers on the ninth ring of hell, we began blind, each of us gradually convinced that we were becoming able to see—license enough for both of us to accuse each other of the worst sins we could think of. Betrayer. Murderer. Beloved.

§

One waiting room after the other, the doctor—dressed up as her own nurse—continually arrives at the appointment time, telling me that the doctor cannot unfortunately make this time due to other commitments, but that the next waiting room is for select patients only, and that the magazines and chairs are better, and in any case you might meet some lovely people among that select few—after all, the doctor is unsurpassed.

§

That small sliver of time between *coitus interruptus* and uneasy sleep, the ever-wilting garden where our mutual adoration blossomed and grew.

§

My trust is born to be betrayed; yours will have never been given. Your bed was a locked trapdoor; my apartment was your midden.

§

Her braid, the metonymy of my desire for her in person. Entranced by the endless knot, I lost track of her face, her body, even her hair. I wonder if we ever broke up; perhaps I've hallucinated everything since.

§

Every attempt to write about her devolved into cliché. Fortunate, then, that her ambitions never exceeded advertising.

§

What lovers have not learnt the geometry of the neck and the wrist, that sacred geometry that breaks the orthogonal into the arcs of love and lust?

§

Still heavy with the silt of your gestures.

I apologise. For many years, I have misunderstood. I pick up your bed and walk.

PREGNANT WITH THE PAST

The body is not an organic unity, but an archipelago. And how many of these islets and coastlines slowly drift away from us ... how far parts of our body are from the rest. What kind of effort would it take to hold them together?

§

Why do we say 'guilty pleasure' when it is rather the guilt that is pleasurable, the picking at the torn quick of the soul? The German *heimliches Vergügen* is a particularly egregious name for the phenomena, given just how public every display of pleasure is, above all when one is alone. Eros never speaks with an inside voice.

§

Think for a moment of speaking to the bourgeois dead: 'I know you suffered terribly, darling, but you weren't married to *Roger* ...' And now, think of all of those good folk waiting for the next life, but codependent on the grift and mediocre cruelty of life on earth. Ah! The golden sheen of gruel! An eternity in the company of your contemporaries? Hell is infinitely to be preferred.

§

The lecturer steeps himself in ease, gradually losing grip on form in favour of content. Their own teachers—singers, audio engineers, actors, deceitful lovers—are forgotten more profoundly each morning.

Consider the shamefully guileless smile as the hush falls, the lazy hand in the pocket, the neanderthal slide decks. Behold! The narcissist who *knows*!

§

The postures of musicians are lessons unlearnt, even, in some cases, by the musicians themselves. Ah, but they do not need to learn them. To notice the school we did not attend is at the same time to notice the school we can no longer. We always learn too late what we did not learn. But: to create is always to create a new school. The general lesson is that grief must be deposed.

§

The perpetration of the human race on itself by itself for itself in itself. Manifold calamity surpassing both tragedy and comedy in its early stages.

§

Utter the cry: martyrs unite! Those who take it up will have given us their measure.

§

Those like Cioran who find in music a proof of some kind listened too briefly and too narrowly. The only thing that music in general assures is sound.

Kant slept. Kant slept, and the years accumulated as they tend to do. The broad but bold lines of the sketch of the world that plastered the inside walls of his trojan horse faded, or were drawn over and reworked by mathematicians and artists. When he finally wakes—who can say when?—all that will be left is the portrait of the neurotic that he always was, in a world that does not understand that it still paints itself and writes its diaries in the ink of his discovery.

§

Arendt's *amor mundi* fragment—you feel like responding as Spinoza's shadow: 'The evidence of the world's love of us is non-existent, therefore we cannot want to love the world.'

§

Arendt wonders why it is so hard to love 'the world'. But the world must not be loved. The world is a screen on which we project anticipated futures, and because it can be anticipated, it belongs to the past. Since it tells us what is already given in advance, it deserves to be the object of a special, *a priori* hatred. Now extrapolate—what does it means when someone declares something, someone, some place 'their world'? Their enjoyment comes from being perpetually washed back into the past, drinking to excess the lotus-flavoured backwash of the past. You must resolutely turn your back on these premature corpses, these betrayers of the night, the truth, the future.

'Euphemism' has become a euphemism for euphemism.

§

Curiousity cannot be found on the line that passes through both perplexity and amusement.

§

Philosophy begins in misery and has its ends in the school; the aphorism begins in despair and has its ends in the brothel.

THE BELTANE LIE

Reading old diary entries today,
Stumbled across the disaster again.
The occasion—a public holiday!—when
The whole edifice suddenly crumbled.

Quote:

> *Oh gods of the earth*, I wearily chanted
> *or the vacant mantic lidless sky, send me*
> *a sign*. (This has to be some kind of apophatic
> Joke I thought: endless set-up, no punchline)
>
> I droned on: *Swing low*
> *sweet Veneris and gently laus down*
> *Somewhere warmer and better lit than*
> *This midtown rental six feet underground.*
>
> Nothing.
>
> I paused for an extra moment,
> Posed arse-up at the altar, waiting
> for the whip, truth's vernacular crack.
> More nothing.
>
> Decades at it, my father's son, and
> His, and so on back into the catalogue.
> All firing the same blanks, the same
> Hollow-point pre-owned thought.
>
> But not that day, my phantasmatic
> posthumous inamorata. I found myself
> setting alight the law suit pursuant to

the missing rib, then drinking hard

and fast to blind the pineal eye,
and blasphemously chirping
like a black hole to the earshotted
on the matter of the beltane lie of hope.

Pinned to the wall by the aghasts' gazes
I thought: silence has never seemed so blessed.

End quote. Pause.

It's been much too long since I've written. Of course,
The aforementioned sense of blessing soon withered
As the hangover flourished with a brutal majesty.
Dead fears from the future made me tremble.

I still teach the syncretic rites—diverting
Gussied-up auto-victimising fist fights,
the lame cavorting with the lame, etc.
Even so, I continue to pray, sounding

'The' Word's *truc* and *trac*, syllables
Counter-stacked to wedge the days
open a little, for the love of not facing
facts: we are just the afterbirth of stars

Meat-hook marionettes spree-shopping
On credit in the strip-mall of time,
Dead days dogging dogged steps.
These are the days of our lives.

DIE HAND

Nature is only the most proximate universal in thought. The error is in thinking it absolute at the same time.

§

As if the syrup left over from the pressing of every popular record had been vapourised.

§

Merleau-Ponty draws attention to the reversibility of the touching and the touched—a hand can change position in relation to the other hand. If you have a moment next time you're masturbating, you can easily determine that it is not a universal phenomenon.

§

The only really basic material fact of human history is rape. Everything else implies it, presupposes it, extrapolates from it. The correlate diagnostic truth about human existence, the truth you do not want to see, is that there is no act of violence—real or imagined—that does not involve pleasure. And now notice how quickly you passed from the fact of rape itself, in its specificity and in the specificity of the intertwining of violence and pleasure that it involves—to a general statement about human conduct, and a thesis about violence. A sentence is enough to make this most basic, most wretched, fact, slip from your hands.

Every house tends towards the coffin.

§

As a regulative ideal, the orgy is indistinguishable from a representation of societal norms.

§

Astonishing and fundamental, the complicity between suicidal thoughts and narcissism. Their shared foundation is a basic aggressivity, a truth long known. But lately, there has been a novel scent emitted from this scene, you can catch a whiff of something sour.

§

To give the suicide of another person a positive moral valence is not the advance in sentimental education that it appears. That death is at the very border of the community, in those fens. A polite formulation of policy and habit that would grant even unexpected suicides 'dignity' is a cheaply perfumed grim, totalising economic fallacy, an attempt to absorb suicide into the shared double-entry book-keeping of the State and consciousness. There must be no talk of responsibility or respect, beyond the simple affirmation of an abeyance of all judgment.

The grey silence of that act deserves nothing. The grief of the ego is eminently understandable, calculable; these days we play at measuring it. Suicide is not.

Beyond good and evil also means—beyond

the narcissistic suffering of the self and beyond reason, beyond the disgusting incorporative gesture of a collective forgiveness that erases the singularity of the name.

At the same time, we must continue to consider suicide one of the highest objects of thought and practice. Without this thought, any thought of political solidarity, any expression of love, any epistemological ideal, any consistency of a work of art is empty, a profound conformity.

§

If there are any moral imperatives, smoking is one. There are many things in the world that deserve to be reduced to ash. We await minor technological developments before we can smoke our household waste; more significant developments will be required in order that we can smoke our regrets, our memories, our incorporated (un)dead.

§

The ticking of mortality's clock is best heard in the fullness of a flourishing act. The more tightly it governs your time, the louder—and *falser*—it sounds itself.

§

You continue to eat—why? Enjoyment of any superior kind is long gone, as is any 'aesthetic' attachment to technique or form. The nutritional function has nothing to do with the matter—the laughable hierarchy of needs is a fiction penned while desire was distracted, her hem, her gaze, etc. All that is left is to take food as daily grime, solyent, gunk, stuff ... but this fact only heightens the mystery. Why continue? What does the mouth know that the rest of the body does not?

§

Rare is the silent person. Most, even in their own company, are talking to themselves, however softly.

§

In belonging nowhere, you discover in your abject, universal belonging. You are the unwanted visitor, the guest who is not welcome, the accident at the dinner table, the sexless, unarousing one night stand. Waste no energy resenting the world, but locate yourself in the heart of its indifference and write that world into life.

What value in loving yourself? None. Being lovable and being loved do not even rank in a different order. Self-love is the snake entranced by a portrait of its own shed skin.

§

The shadow cast by a figure in a mirror, the self is not a possible object of love.

§

Hardly any exception: the great urban monographs are biographical in character, the city appearing as a variegated screen upon which smaller matters are projected—Burroughs' Tangiers, Lowry's Quauhnahuac.

§

The history of the cinema is the slow digestion of form by content. The steadicam, for instance, functions to reinstate the human bodily relation to perception within the image.

§

There are no cynical pessimists. The cynic is a self-deceiving optimist of a low grade. Pessimism excludes any cynicism, embracing the present state with equanimity. The cynic is opposed not by the *naif*, but by the person honest and self-aware enough to realise that the cynical position is a costume, a carnival mask.

§

The noosphere—the great billboard of the mind—has always been the realm of advertising. Every habituated operation of thought and writing operate upon its surface.

§

Puns, metaphors, metonyms, just like our habits of gesturing, smiling, standing, are all slogans.

§

Perhaps we owe astrophysics a debt of gratitude for some of their clumsy terminology. A rocket's 'stages' seem—at the very least—to supplement the suite of Freudian-Kleinian categories. We can recognise, for instance, the propulsive force of a teenage and post-teenage 'stage' in breaking with the febrile habits of the previous generation. As always, the difficult second stage determines the significance of the first *a tergo.*

§

Find within yourself the fantasy of an absolute desert, an absolute nowhere. In that desert you will find your true self, an absolute no-one—a shadow that interrupts the lines of the sand in the daytime, and a canvas for the light of the moon at night. Remember this place. It is the only salvation that can be found on your own terms.

There is no silence; silence is a fantasy. Everyone and everything mutters beneath its breath. This is why you get so little sleep.

§

The blind-side of anarchism: gods and masters continually whip past on the left into the rear-vision, while you read about it on your phone.

§

An existentialism of colours. Abandon the ideal of being yourself—foolish, trivial, familial—and simply strive towards colourism.

§

The difference between technical proficiency and artistry is not the degree of imagination imbued in the latter—the deployment of imagination is itself a technique.

§

Sin seduces because the sun shines. Seduction is a sin because the sun shines. The sun shines because sin ...

§

Seduction is the only process capable of discriminating between sincerity and boredom at the root. That we can take anything sincerely—responsibility, writing, belief, love—is due to the fact of seduction.

Fortunate, the small size of our eyes. A few millimetres larger and human existence would be simply impossible.

§

Grief, and its terrifying force, can be our teacher—of the meaning of a breath, the capacity to stand from a chair, conclude a sentence. It is our cowardice that makes it our injury.

§

The sea is mercy—a gift of a movement of endless grieving that teaches the wisdom of living and thinking at the same time.

§

As we convalesce from the great plague of bad philosophy, bad science, we rediscover the beautiful sweet levity of error, find again the kind laughter that belongs to simply being wrong.

§

Romance is not dead, but undying. The candied narcissism of our lover's discourse has proven too hard to crack for all but the most vampiric—those trash-can gourmets of the spirit—or those who are willing to suck on it long enough for the poisonous, soporific core to register on the tongue. 'Step down again into the coffin of the simple soul, my beloved'.

As soon as they reach physical 'maturity', men ought to simply ejaculate themselves to death, offering to the soil and to the time of women their greatest gift. Even this seems strictly beyond them, busy as they are with their mewing confessions concerning the facsimiles of feelings they have accidentally entertained, with stories about the fardels they have borne, are bearing, will bear, may bear, will never bear but fear they may nevertheless, would have borne but for the fact they felt they were the symptom of something else, have borne but suspected were not properly weighted, should bear, *should not bear.* Incapable of even embracing their own tribal time-borne wisdom: *you should always use the right tool for the right job.*

§

Extrapolate the exercise of historical study across the course of history itself and its nature reveals itself—a daydreaming so profound it forgets the soil that historians a year from now will take to require unearthing. But these historians, their magic derived from the same shared reverence to the dimension of the past, work with the same featureless ancient tool. They presuppose a lingua franca for time itself, its irreducible fragments. Historians pass off the felt of history for the tapestry of time. Priests of a god without a name, their authority becomes more and more absolute, the greater the secularisation of information. Soon enough, *Angelus Novus* will need to speak up.

The combat of hungers clears space for action.

§

The indifference of lust leads, over some period, to erotic fixation. A boring observation, perhaps. But what existential drift accounts for their coincidence?

§

How loneliness pools, dampens, wearies. It is one of the great liquid phenomena in human experience, down to the experience of drying-off.

§

Velvet looks blacker than straight fabric by distracting the light.

§

Is despair the cocoon of love, or its shed skin? Impossible to say—though this alternative exhausts their possible relationship.

§

Being has no measure. Things are absolute monsters, each time. Except for desire, which gives their smile back to the universe in the form of an absolute rule.

More than any other punctuation mark, the semi-colon must be correctly *felt*. The reader must feel, implied in it, a secret world; the writer must feel in it a tension of the right degree.

§

How poorly the lesson learnt in the dim light of their bedrooms are learnt—between what your eyes know, and your hands is complete.

§

Learn to raise your chin—not just to look at the world anew, but to force a gap between you and its preconceptions.

BURIAL AT SEA

Your face learnt hers when she struggled not to weep; you learnt a habit of mourning. And now, in every grief, she is there with you, and the grief is amplified, unbearably, in this reflection.

§

Exotropia. All romantic songs about relationships treat the during or the after. Songs that try to speak of the breakup are lies that lean forward or backwards. The moment itself—like all moments—is best captured by a purely sonorous relation, which, in its sonorous duration, slips from under every name.

§

The absolute tyranny of affect ... Imagine being *in favour of feeling* as a matter of principle! Not a moment passes when we do not feel. Even numbness has its own modalities, degrees, colours, its own numbnesses. Consequently: there is no difference between the champions of affect and the grammar police. That we should *praise affect as such?* Might as well volunteer to use your pirated copy of pre-subscription Photoshop to produce recruiting flyers for the police.

§

Imagine how much actual work we'd get done if we were not constantly burdened with the requirement to lie at such lengths to make room. Including, of course, the lies we tell to ourselves.

§

Jack Gilbert. Nobody has ever given more to us in the word 'that'.

§

Strange, the ubiquitous belief in the smoothness of the line of the horizon, the confection of its purity. It is never a line but a texture. Related phenomenon: the alleged homogeneity of noise.

§

As the spectre of the apocalypse steadily gains flesh, there now appears on the near horizon the prospect of the last book.

§

Doing is the only tried and true temporary reprieve from *being*. Curse those who work to identify them.

§

Why your apparent fascination for cosmological metaphors, all this talk of stars, space, light? Are you auditioning—to a literally empty cosmic theatre—to be a celestial being?

It is impossible to maintain a pretence if you are impatient for it to be discovered.

Hunger is *sated*, but anger *slaked* like thirst. What other thirsts can be slaked?

§

Forgiving feels much like swallowing. Perhaps this explains the outsized significance of the blowjob in the male imaginarium.

§

Which is worse: mispronouncing a name or misspeling it?

§

No doubt a sentient sea creature would fear falling up out of the depths. To be conscious is just to be (erroneously) cognisant of a displaced spectre of consciousness itself.

§

What explains Plato's fixation on the most obsequious of animals, the dog? By his side, they become wisdom's friend's best man.

Write and then know. Writing in order to be known is a truly psychotic arrangement, analogous to the hope that smiling will make you visible.

§

Disappointment, the tepid bath of the soul—how much more comfortable it is than satisfaction. It is, precisely, the temperature of one's own urine.

§

The being of language is nothing but language's own opalescence in relation to itself.

§

Nothing worse for your procrastination than to collaborate with a confection made of the same stuff. And once it becomes clear that culture in general is little more than an attempt to procrastinate about the fact of death, one wonders why time itself isn't moving backwards. But if it did, the *ratio existendi* for procrastination would itself evaporate

§

For all the intensity of his dark light, Cioran remains a believer in nations. How strange for this most solitary thinker, the true sage of the twentieth century, to continually exercise himself on this most redundant of congenital attachments. He seems to remain convinced that the privileged objects of examination lie in the middle distance.

The idea that somehow death itself can be conquered is the inert and scentless flatulence of the ego. Should the human body somehow be transcended, there will always be the analogue of the puddle, the noise, the slip, the unexpected message, the uneven paving. Death is not fate but contingency, the God of gods and slugs like you alike.

§

Fate is no leash or rope; it is a nest of tripwires.

§

Liberalism's denunciations—as effective as a professor emeritus burbling about the quiet dignity of meter at an orgy.

§

Sex and books—both exist at the point of inflection between the silent frenzy of narcissism and the hunger for threat.

The difference between Arendt's *"Amor mundi—warum ist es so schwer, die Welt zu lieben?"* and Christ's *"E'li, E'li, la-ma sa-bach-tha-ni?"* is endlessly instructive. Hard to overlook what they share though, both being quotations.

Is all that we are left with? The plumbing of the nooks of language, the spelunking of the long, guilty entrails of meaning?

§

Avoid the temptation to identify an horizon with exhaustion. Exhaustion is a byproduct of activity, not an inevitable, unchosen orientation or terminus.

§

The imaginarium is the best map of the interior of consciousness—which is to say, bourgeois consciousness.

§

In the future, children will 'imprint' on a genre of 'reality' television show. Parents, level one content providers, will no longer be responsible, but for their nutrient support.

§

Ah, the taste-makers of nineteenth century ... imagine their utter bemusement if they had known that the figure of the disciplined creator in the late twentieth century would end up being ... the chef.

§

Is it too obvious to note? There is no sound that cannot be socialised. But the lesson of the scream is that this always takes place retroactively.

§

When composing for an orchestra, doubling the seventh is discouraged, due to the shifting harmonic relationship that it holds with the tonic from one instrument to the next. A moral lesson here: decline from approaching a threshold of transformation with someone else also at such a point of inflection.

§

Could it be that insomnia, the most excruciating experience of a heavy nothing, arises from that nil point where boredom with oneself and boredom with the world become indiscernible?

§

Desire is first shared form and not private content—which is to say, the unfolding of a gesture without a single agent, a gesture whose only true secret is what it obscures as it unfolds.

§

Nothing easier than judging the regular denigrations of self-worth in trivial terms. And it is true that the mewing cry 'I'm not good enough' marks the low tide of contemporary culture. Nevertheless, the problem lies not with the adjudicators, but in the misrecognition of 'self-worth' as a meaningful discriminatory scale as such. The medium is the parasite.

The world is the Port au Prince, has always been. The sea, the land, the murderer, the impatient sand, the free, the threat, the cruel blind, the blindly cruel, the double bind, the past. The future.

§

Certitude is an affect, at most a characteristic of behaviour. It bears no epistemological significance.

§

Tattoos tell the truth of a person the way that figured bass implies chords.

§

Love does not banish fear, but excretes it.

§

You repeat the same ideas, anxieties, really, over and over again in these books—Certainly. But what else am I supposed to do? And in any case, you keep reading them.

§

Learn a language on the condition you would never speak it. Cold and dark, it would lie still within your body, watching your gestures, your failed words and your failed loves. Your restlessness and desperation. Your inability to take pleasure in anything. Cremated after you die, the words will lay amongst the ashes as they fall into the depths of the sea, watching the world from underneath until all of the light goes out.

THE ROPE KITE

Around that flaxen ourobouros
I've carefully run my gaze, twice, three times
Not quite a perfect circle
But the more alluring for its eccentricity
Eye and mind both fit it snugly
From the right distance

This thing I had tied myself
I mean, by myself and for myself
Hangs before me, here, in this small room
A terrible thought looming over its thin shadow
A mute premonition of consequence
Stiller than any conviction

That shadow can seem the opening
Gambit of an illuminated manuscript
But the thing itself appears to be
A ladder, an empty storeroom, a bridge
Or the long, lonely rope wrist of an anchor
Lost in seas too heavy for it

But tilt your head and you might see it right
It's the bare frame of a kite hanging upside-down
The skeleton of a beast of flight
The embryo of every escape
True, not many ever see it this way
Make one yourself and you will.

Read about it: the molecules in a brick
Unlatched can destroy a city
This slip of a thing, certainly less

Though still exactly too much
Unwound, its threads would reach a mile
Tied just like this, much further.

The rope kite, alone among its brethren
Belongs to earth as well as air,
Is one means of reconciling this quarreling couple
Like its dear sisters, it is at its stillest
Before it takes off, while it waits,
And at the apex of its flight. Between, it trembles.

Some days, I long for it to catch me up
And throw me joyously into the sky
To punch the wind out of my weak lungs.
On others, for its one strong arm
To hold me firm and calm near cold soil
To pack night into my bent bones.

Lately, though, I simply entertain its slim
Silhouette in the corner of my eye, while
All my hours hang, like the kite,
Between atmosphere and earth
The interregnal friction not yet charged enough
To set that rope machine to work.

www.ingramcontent.com/pod-product-compliance
Lightning Source LLC
La Vergne TN
LVHW051014080826
845145LV00009B/2615
* 9 7 8 1 7 6 4 2 3 4 6 3 4 *